POCKET MANUAL

Teams and players, facts and figures

WORLD CUP FOOTBALL

Jason Ludditch has asserted his right to be identified as the
author of this book.

Published in April 2010.

British Library Cataloguing-in-Publication Data:
A catalogue record for this book is available from
the British Library

ISBN 978 1 84425 964 9

Published by Haynes Publishing,
Sparkford, Yeovil, Somerset BA22 7JJ, UK
Tel: 01963 442030 Fax: 01963 440001
Int. tel: +44 1963 442030 Int. fax: +44 1963 440001
Email: sales@haynes.co.uk
Website: www.haynes.co.uk

Haynes North America, Inc.,
861 Lawrence Drive, Newbury Park
California 91320, USA

Design and layout by Richard Parsons

All photographs courtesy of Getty Images

All statistics and dates correct as of 9 January 2010

Printed in the USA

The Author

Jason Ludditch, who has written for *Hotspur*, the *Evertonian* and
FourFourTwo, remembers Mexico '86 as the first World Cup he
ever watched. As an eight-year-old, he cried after England were
knocked out by Argentina. He's hoping he won't be crying this year.

POCKET MANUAL

Teams and players, facts and figures

WORLD CUP FOOTBALL

WORLD CUP FOOTBALL
CONTENTS

ONES TO WATCH   72

From great goalkeepers to fearsome forwards, we pick more potential stars

RISING STARS   88

The finest young talent looking to impress and make their mark in South Africa

WORLD CUPS   96

From 1930 to 2006, re-live the winners, losers and best bits from all 18 World Cup tournaments so far

LEGENDS   116

The players that have been there, done it and left their mark on the world's biggest stage

FREE STATE STADIUM

CITY: Bloemfontein CAPACITY: 48,000

ROYAL BAFOKENG STADIUM

CITY: Rustenburg CAPACITY: 42,000

PORT ELIZABETH STADIUM

CITY: Port Elizabeth CAPACITY: 48,000

GREEN POINT STADIUM

CITY: Cape Town CAPACITY: 70,000

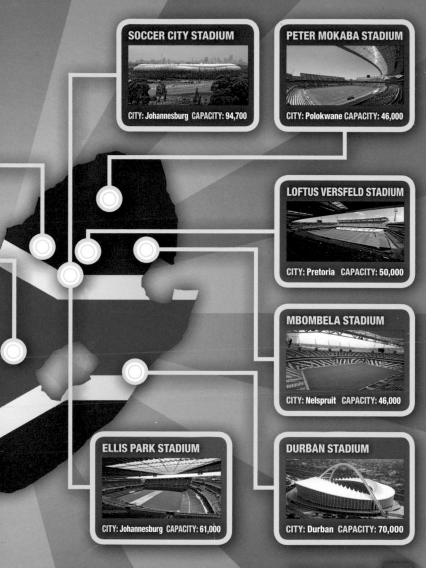

SOCCER CITY STADIUM

CITY: Johannesburg CAPACITY: 94,700

PETER MOKABA STADIUM

CITY: Polokwane CAPACITY: 46,000

LOFTUS VERSFELD STADIUM

CITY: Pretoria CAPACITY: 50,000

MBOMBELA STADIUM

CITY: Nelspruit CAPACITY: 46,000

ELLIS PARK STADIUM

CITY: Johannesburg CAPACITY: 61,000

DURBAN STADIUM

CITY: Durban CAPACITY: 70,000

SOUTH AFRICA

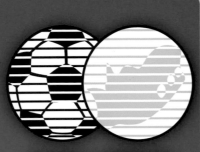

SOUTH AFRICAN
FOOTBALL ASSOCIATION

COACH:
Carlos Alberto Parreira

WORLD CUP RECORD:
1998: Round 1,
2002: Round 1

MOST CAPPED PLAYER:
Aaron Mokoena (97)

TOP GOALSCORER:
Benni McCarthy (32)

South Africa hold the distinction of being the first nation to participate in a qualifying competition despite hosting the tournament. They were guaranteed a place in the finals, but because the preliminaries served to qualify teams for the Africa Cup of Nations as well, they were required to take part. The nation was re-admitted to FIFA in 1993 after a lengthy ban. After winning the Africa Cup of Nations in 1996, they qualified for the 1998 and 2002 World Cups. They also hosted the FIFA Confederations Cup in 2009, in which they finished fourth after losing a play-off against Spain.

STEVEN PIENAAR

BORN: 17/03/1982
POSITION: Midfield
CAPS: 47
GOALS: 2

The Everton midfielder was voted South Africa's footballer of the year for 2009 by South African football fans. Pienaar grew up in what used to be a township on the edge of Johannesburg and, should he walk out as part of the South African team that kicks off this summer's opening game, it will be at the Soccer City stadium in Soweto, a stone's throw from where his mother lives. Pienaar enjoyed an impressive 2009 for Everton, whom he joined on loan before signing on a permanent deal from Borussia Dortmund.

MEXICO

COACH: Javier Aguirre

WORLD CUP RECORD: 1930: Round 1, 1950: Round 1, 1954: Round 1, 1958: Round 1, 1962: Round 1, 1966: Round 1, 1970: Quarter-finals, 1978: Round 1, 1986: Quarter-finals, 1994: Last 16, 1998: Last 16, 2002: Last 16, 2006: Last 16

MOST CAPPED PLAYER: Claudio Suárez (178)

TOP GOALSCORER: Jared Borgetti (46)

Mexico have had three managers and more than 60 players in the last three years. Yet after negotiating their qualifying group with five consecutive wins against their group opponents under new boss Javier Aguirre, *El Tri* will be looking to progress beyond the Last 16 for the first time since 1986. Mexico have twice reached the quarter-finals of the World Cup – they were hosts on both occasions, in 1970 and 1986. Now, with members of their 2005 Under-17 World Cup winners combining with more experienced players in the senior team, many consider the current combination a 'golden generation'.

RAFAEL MARQUEZ

BORN: 13/02/1979
POSITION: Defence
CAPS: 87
GOALS: 10

The two-time Champions League winner was key to Mexico overcoming a terrible start to their qualification campaign and finishing second in the CONCACAF zone. Marquez won the FIFA Confederations Cup in 1999 and the CONCACAF Gold Cup the same year and he has appeared in two World Cup competitions. In 2002 he was given the captain's armband for the first time, at the age of 23. Despite being sent off in a last-16 defeat against USA, he returned four years later and was ever-present.

URUGUAY

COACH: Oscar Tabarez

WORLD CUP RECORD: 1930: Champions, 1950: Champions, 1954: Fourth place, 1962: Round 1, 1966: Quarter-finals, 1970: Fourth place, 1974: Round 1, 1986: Last 16, 1990: Last 16, 2002: Round 1

MOST CAPPED PLAYER:
Rodolfo Rodríguez (79)

TOP GOALSCORER: Héctor Scarone (31)

Uruguay have made just two appearances at the last five FIFA World Cups, but they boast an enviable record in the competition. *La Celeste* hosted – and won – the inaugural finals in 1930, beating Argentina 4-2 in the final. They triumphed again in 1950 in Brazil, made the quarter-finals in 1966 and finished fourth in 1970. They have failed to make it past the last 16 since. This will be their 11th appearance at the finals. Their place was secured via a two-legged play-off win against Costa Rica after they finished fifth in the CONMEBOL zone.

STAR MAN

DIEGO FORLAN

BORN: 19/05/1979
POSITION: Forward
CAPS: 60
GOALS: 22

Diego Forlan has followed in the footsteps of his father, who represented Uruguay, and his grandfather, who played for Argentine giants Independiente. He started his career with *El Rojo* and has netted 22 goals in 58 internationals, seven of which helped Uruguay qualify for South Africa. After moving to Spain in 2004 he scored 54 goals in 106 games for Villarreal. In 2009 he was awarded the European Golden Shoe and the Pichichi Trophy after scoring 32 goals in 33 La Liga appearances for Atletico Madrid.

FRANCE

COACH: Raymond Domenech

WORLD CUP RECORD: 1930: Round 1, 1934: Round 1, 1938: Quarter-finals, 1954: Round 1, 1958: Third place, 1966: Round 1, 1978: Round 1, 1982: Fourth place, 1986: Third place, 1998: Winners, 2002: Round 1, 2006: Runners-up

MOST CAPPED PLAYER:
Lilian Thuram (142)

TOP GOALSCORER: Thierry Henry (51)

One of four European teams to compete in the inaugural World Cup in 1930, France boast a fine record in the competition. The first of two European Championship triumphs in 1984 was sandwiched between two World Cup semi-finals, but they finally added the biggest prize of all to their collection in 1998, when they beat Brazil on home soil. They won the European Championship again in 2000 to become the first national team to hold both the World and European titles since West Germany in 1974. This is the first time they have qualified for four consecutive World Cups.

NICOLAS ANELKA

BORN: 14/03/1979
POSITION: Forward
CAPS: 63
GOALS: 13

The second most expensive player in the world as a result of his cumulative transfer fees, Anelka has played 29 of France's last 37 internationals. He made his international debut in April 1998 but didn't feature in the World Cup that year. He had to wait until Euro 2000 to make his major tournament bow, while his failure to settle at one club and subsequent loss of form saw him miss out on adding to his cap tally between the Confederations Cup in 2001 and September 2007.

ARGENTINA

COACH: Diego Maradona

WORLD CUP RECORD: 1930: Finalists, 1934: Round 1, 1958: Round 1, 1962: Round 1, 1966: Quarter-finals, 1974: Round 2, 1978: Winners, 1982: Last 16, 1986: Winners, 1990: Runners-up, 1994: Last 16, 1998: Quarter-finals. 2002: Round 1, 2006: Quarter-finals

MOST CAPPED PLAYER: Javier Zanetti (136)

TOP GOALSCORER: Gabriel Batistuta (56)

Argentina endured a nerve-jangling climax to their qualifying campaign. Slender wins against Peru and Uruguay secured the *Albicelestes'* 10th consecutive appearance in the World Cup, and they head to South Africa looking to win the tournament for the first time in 24 years. Argentina were involved in the first World Cup final in 1930, where they lost to hosts Uruguay. They won the trophy twice in eight years, first in 1978, defeating the Netherlands and again in 1986, beating West Germany in Mexico. The Germans gained revenge four years later, when they beat Argentina 1-0 in Italy.

LIONEL MESSI

BORN: 24/06/1987
POSITION: Forward
CAPS: 44
GOALS: 13

After impressing at Under-20 level, where he was part of the FIFA World Youth Championship winning team in 2005 and won both the Golden Ball and Golden Shoe Awards, Messi made his full debut in 2005, against Hungary. He became the youngest player to represent his country at the World Cup when he came on as a substitute against Serbia in 2006, and his goal in the 6-0 win made him the youngest scorer in that competition, the fourth youngest in tournament history.

COACH: Shaibu Amodu

WORLD CUP RECORD:
1994: Last 16,
1998: Last 16,
2002: Round 1

MOST CAPPED PLAYER:
Mudashiru Lawal (86)

TOP GOALSCORER:
Rashidi Yekini (37)

The two times Africa Cup of Nations winners made up for the disappointment of missing out on the World Cup in 2006 by topping a group including Tunisia, Mozambique and Kenya to qualify for South Africa. It will be the *Super Eagles'* fourth World Cup. In 1994, they made it to the last 16 at the first attempt, topping their group ahead of Argentina. They eventually lost to finalists Italy, but they repeated the feat four years later, when Spain succumbed to the Nigerians' power. Denmark proved too strong in the second round. They went out in the group stages in 2002.

STAR MAN

OBAFEMI MARTINS

BORN: 28/10/1984
POSITION: Forward
CAPS: 26
GOALS: 15

With 15 goals in 26 international appearances, Martins poses the biggest threat for the *Super Eagles*. A sprint champion as a youngster, Martins adds a prolific eye for goal and a penchant for the spectacular to his electrifying speed. He missed nine of Nigeria's 12 qualifiers through injury, but returned for the final game against Kenya, scoring twice. Martins scored 28 goals in 87 league games in Italy before he moved to Newcastle United in 2006. After three seasons at St James' Park, he moved to German side Wolfsburg.

SOUTH KOREA

COACH: Huh Jung-Moo

WORLD CUP RECORD:
1954: Round 1, 1986: Round 1,
1990: Round 1, 1994: Round 1, 1998:
Round 1, 2002: Fourth, 2006: Round 1

MOST CAPPED PLAYER:
Hong Myung-Bo (136)

TOP GOALSCORER:
Cha Bum-Kun (55)

The *Red Devils* are making their seventh successive appearance at the World Cup finals after topping their group ahead of rivals Korea DPR. Their neighbours finished second, but South Korea failed to beat them in two attempts. Their fourth-place finish in 2002 remains their best so far – they co-hosted the tournament with Japan and beat Portugal, Italy and Spain en route to reaching the semi-finals, where they lost to Germany. South Korea have long been the dominant force in Asian football and they were the first Asian team to make it to the finals, reaching Switzerland in 1954.

PARK JI-SUNG

BORN: 25/02/1981
POSITION: Midfield
CAPS: 85
GOALS: 11

The Manchester United winger played the most minutes of any player in South Korea's qualifying campaign, and top scored with five goals. He started his international career aged just 19 as a defensive midfielder, but it was not until he played under former coach Guus Hiddink that he reached his best form. Park proved his versatility, playing wide left or right or as an attacking central midfielder. He scored the winning goal that saw Korea beat Portugal in the decisive group match at the World Cup in 2002.

GREECE

ΕΛΛΑΣ

COACH:
Otto Rehhagel

WORLD CUP RECORD:
1994: Round 1

MOST CAPPED PLAYER:
Theodoros Zagorakis (120)

TOP GOALSCORER:
Nikos Anastopoulos (29)

The defining moment in Greek football came at Euro 2004. Dismissed as rank outsiders in Portugal, they not only reached the final after knocking out defending champions France, they also beat the hosts 1-0 in one of international football's biggest shocks. This was only their second appearance in the European Championship, a disappointing third followed in 2008, while their appearance in South Africa – courtesy of a play-off win against Ukraine – will be their second in the World Cup. Their first and only appearance came in 1994, when they lost three games and conceded 10 goals without scoring.

THEOFANIS GEKAS

BORN: 23/05/1980
POSITION: Forward
CAPS: 45
GOALS: 20

The Larissa-born striker has been in fine form for his country despite struggling for games, first during a recent loan spell at Portsmouth and again on his return to Bayer Leverkusen. He scored 10 of Greece's 20 goals in qualifying – more than any other player in the European zone. He first came into the side after his country's shock triumph in Euro 2004 and finished top scorer in Greece with 17 goals in 2005 while playing for Panathinaikos. He moved to German side Bochum in 2006, then a year later joined Leverkusen.

ENGLAND

ENGLAND

COACH: Fabio Capello

WORLD CUP RECORD: 1950: Round 1, 1954: Quarter-finals, 1958: Round 1, 1962: Quarter-finals, 1966: Winners, 1970: Quarter-finals, 1982: Last 16, 1986: Quarter-finals, 1990: fourth place, 1998: round 2, 2002: Quarter-finals, 2006: Quarter-finals

MOST CAPPED PLAYER: Peter Shilton (125)

TOP GOALSCORER: Sir Bobby Charlton (49)

England are one of seven teams to have won the World Cup. The *Three Lions* went all the way on home soil in 1966, a Geoff Hurst hat-trick in the final help beat West Germany in a 4-2 thriller at Wembley, remembered for a controversial goal that cannoned off the crossbar before being adjudged to have crossed the line. England have qualified for 10 tournaments since their first in 1950. The closest they have come to winning it a second time was in Italy in 1990, when West Germany beat them on penalties in the semi-finals.

WAYNE ROONEY

BORN: 24/10/1985
POSITION: Forward
CAPS: 57
GOALS: 25

Wayne Rooney has been breaking records ever since he pulled on an England shirt. With his first cap, against Australia in 2003, he became the youngest England player aged just 17. In 2004, at the European Championship in Portugal, he became the youngest scorer in competition history when he found the net against Switzerland. More recently, as England qualified as top scorers in Europe with 34 goals, he became the first England player to score 10 goals in a single season since Gary Lineker in 1990/91.

COACH: Bob Bradley

WORLD CUP RECORD: 1930: Third, 1934: Round 1, 1950: Round 1, 1990: Round 1, 1994: Round 1, 1998: Round 1, 2002: Quarter-finals, 2006: Round 1

MOST CAPPED PLAYER:
Cobi Jones (164)

TOP GOALSCORER:
Landon Donovan (42)

USA topped the CONCACAF qualifying zone to ensure a sixth consecutive place at the finals, their ninth in total. Earlier in 2009 they finished second at the FIFA Confederations Cup in South Africa. They beat Spain on the way to the final, inflicting *La Roja's* first defeat in 35 games before losing to Brazil. The USA finished fourth in the first World Cup in 1930 and shocked the world 20 years later by beating England 1-0 in Chile. Their best finish since a semi-final bow in Uruguay came in 2002, when they were knocked out in the quarter-finals by runners up Germany.

LANDON DONOVAN

BORN: 04/03/1982
POSITION: Forward
CAPS: 120
GOALS: 42

The holder of the most caps in the existing US squad, it was Donovan's goal against Honduras that clinched his side's place in South Africa. He boasts World Cup experience from 2006, when the States were eliminated from the group stage. He scored 35 goals in 41 games for the USA's under-20 side, earning a call-up to the Under-23 squad in 2000 and a full cap in October, when he scored on his debut against Mexico. In October 2008 he scored his 35th goal and overtook Eric Wynalda as the *Stars and Stripes'* highest scorer of all time.

ALGERIA

COACH:
Rabah Saddane

WORLD CUP RECORD:
1982: Round 1,
1986: Round 1

MOST CAPPED PLAYER:
Mahieddine Meftah (107)

TOP GOALSCORER:
Abdelhafid Rasfaout (35)

Algeria knocked out rivals Egypt in a play-off match to qualify for their first World Cup in 24 years. After forming in 1958, *Les Fennecs* failed to qualify for a major tournament until consecutive World Cups in the 1980s. In 1982, they upset European champions West Germany, beating them 2-1. They also beat Chile but were knocked out at the first hurdle after losing to Austria in their final group game. They were knocked out in the first round four years later in Mexico, before winning the Africa Cup of Nations in 1990.

STAR MAN

KARIM ZIANI

BORN: 17/08/1982
POSITION: Midfield
CAPS: 46
GOALS: 4

The midfielder was ever-present in qualifying and finished as joint-top scorer alongside Rafik Saifi and Antar Yahia, with three goals. His willingness to get forward makes him a creative threat, and he was particularly impressive in the crucial group wins against Egypt, Zambia and Rwanda. He scored his first international goal in 2008 in a 1-0 win against Gambia in the Africa Cup of Nations. Four years earlier, Ziani starred in the competition in Tunisia, and was voted best player in his position.

SLOVENIA

SLOVENIJA
NZS

COACH:
Matjaž Kek

WORLD CUP RECORD:
2002: Round 1

MOST CAPPED PLAYER:
Zlatko Zahovic (80)

TOP GOALSCORER:
Zlatko Zahovic (35)

Matjaz Kek's Slovenia side have written a new chapter in the nation's brief sporting history merely by qualifying for this World Cup. They finished ahead of the Czech Republic and Poland before shocking Russia in the play-offs. After declaring independence in 1991, the country has qualified for two major tournaments. They impressed during Euro 2000 after beating Ukraine in a play-off and played good football despite finishing bottom of Group A, which included Spain, Yugoslavia and Norway. They reached the World Cup two years later, but again went out in the first round.

ROBERT KOREN

BORN: 20/09/1980
POSITION: Midfield
CAPS: 44
GOALS: 4

The West Bromwich Albion playmaker forms the creative hub of Slovenia's midfield, breaking up attacks in front of Samir Handanovic in goal and providing the ammunition for Milivoje Novakovic in attack. Koren missed just two games in qualifying and he will lead his side into South Africa as captain. His playing style has seen him compared to former skipper Zlatko Zahovic, who holds the record for most caps and goals for his country. Koren joined the Baggies from Norwegian side Lillestrom in 2007.

GERMANY

COACH: Joachim Low

WORLD CUP RECORD: 1930: withdrew, 1934: Third place, 1938: Round 1, 1954: Winners, 1958: Fourth place, 1962: Quarter-finals, 1966: Runners-up, 1970: Third place, 1974: Winners, 1978: Last 16, 1982: Runners-up, 1986: Runners-up, 1990: Winners, 1994: Quarter-finals, 1998: Quarter-finals, 2002: Runners-up, 2006: Third place

MOST CAPPED PLAYER: Lothar Matthäus (150)

TOP GOALSCORER: Gerd Müller (68)

Germany boast a glorious record in the World Cup and have appeared in all but two tournaments. Their first triumph came in 1954, in Switzerland, and they added a second on home soil 20 years later. Franz Beckenbauer, who captained the side to glory in 1974, then coached the team to their most recent victory, in 1990. His side beat Argentina after having lost the previous two finals. Third in 2006 and second at the European Championship two years later, they will be looking to complete the sequence and go one better in South Africa and return to the winners' podium.

MIROSLAV KLOSE

BORN: 09/06/1978
POSITION: Forward
CAPS: 93
GOALS: 48

Poland-born Klose uses his father's German nationality to represent *Die Mannschaft*, for whom he has played in two major finals. He picked up a runners-up medal in the 2002 World Cup and another at Euro 2008. He narrowly missed out on another World Cup final in 2006, when Germany were beaten by Brazil in the semi-finals. Second in the all-time list of World Cup goalscorers alongside compatriots Rudi Voller and Jurgen Klinsmann, Klose is six goals short of becoming the highest in history.

FOOTBALL FEDERATION AUSTRALIA

COACH: Pim Verbeek

WORLD CUP RECORD:
1974: Round 1,
2006: Last 16

MOST CAPPED PLAYER:
Alex Tobin (87)

TOP GOALSCORER:
Damiean Mori (29)

Australia have played in two previous World Cup tournaments. Their first appearance came in West Germany in 1974, where they went out in the first round after losing against East and West Germany and drawing with Chile. Thirty-two years later, again in Germany, they emerged from a group including Brazil and Croatia to make the last 16, where they narrowly lost to eventual winners Italy. This time, instead of their usual qualifying route, they emerged victorious from the Asian zone after having joined the Asian Football Confederation in 2006.

MARK SCHWARZER

BORN: 06/10/1972
POSITION: Goalkeeper
CAPS: 72
GOALS: 0

The 37-year-old was rewarded for his part in helping the *Socceroos* qualify for the World Cup when he was awarded the Medal of the Order of Australia in 2009. Schwarzer let in just four goals and enjoyed a national record of seven matches without conceding. Schwarzer – Fulham's Player of the Year in 2008/09 – was also instrumental when Australia qualified for the World Cup four years previously. He saved two penalties in a 4-2 win against Uruguay in the play-offs.

CPБИJA

COACH: Radomir Anti

WORLD CUP RECORD: As Yugoslavia: 1930: Fourth place, 1950: Round 1, 1954: Quarter-finals, 1958: Quarter-finals, 1962: Fourth place, 1974: Round 2, 1982: Round 1, 1990: Quarter-finals, 1998: Last 16: As Serbia & Montengro: 2006: Round 1

MOST CAPPED PLAYER: Savo Miloševic (102)

TOP GOALSCORER: Stjepan Bobek (38)

South Africa represents Serbia's first appearance at a World Cup as an independent state. They beat France, Romania and Austria to top their group in qualifying. *Beli Orlovi* appeared under the banner of Yugoslavia until 2003. They reached the semi-finals in 1930 and qualified for nine tournaments before achieving independence in 2003. Serbia and Montenegro qualified to play in Germany in 2006 before the two states split. Serbia played their first international independently on August 16 2006, beating the Czech Republic 3-1.

DEJAN STANKOVIC

BORN: 11/09/1978
POSITION: Midfield
CAPS: 85
GOALS: 13

Stankovic made his international debut for what was FR Yugoslavia against South Korea in April of 1998, represented Serbia and Montenegro in 2006 in Germany before captaining the current side to success in the recent qualifiers. Stankovic was ever-present until injury kept him out of the last two games. The Belgrade-born attacking midfielder plays for Internazionale in Italy. A creative playmaker, his passing ability and shooting prowess have made him one of Europe's most skilful performers.

GHANA

GHANA FOOTBALL ASSOCIATION

COACH:
Milovan Rajevac

WORLD CUP RECORD:
2006: Last 16

MOST CAPPED PLAYER:
Abedi Pele (73)

TOP GOALSCORER:
Abedi Pele (33)

After waiting 44 years to qualify for their first World Cup, Ghana made it two in a row by topping their group on goal difference ahead of Libya and Gabon, becoming the first African side to qualify for South Africa. In Germany, in 2006, they were the only African side to make it to the knockout stages. They were eventually knocked out by Brazil in the last 16. Ghana have won four Africa Cup of Nations titles, two Under-17 World Cups and in October 2009, they added the Under-20 World Cup to their trophy cabinet.

STAR MAN

MICHAEL ESSIEN

BORN: 03/12/1982
POSITION: Midfield
CAPS: 50
GOALS: 9

Michael Essien's energy, physical presence and ability to score from distance have made him a key player for club and country. He played in 11 of Ghana's 12 qualifying matches and scored one of the two goals against Sudan that helped his side clinch the first African spot in the finals. He was instrumental as Ghana reached the last 16 in 2006, and he was sorely missed when they lost 3-0 to eventual winners Brazil. Essien joined Chelsea from Olympique Lyonnais for £24.4 million in 2005.

NETHERLANDS

COACH: Bert van Marwijk

WORLD CUP RECORD:
1934: Round 1, 1938: Round 1, 1974:
Runners-up, 1978: Runners-up, 1990:
Last 16, 1994: Quarter-finals, 1998:
Quarter-finals, 2006: Last 16

MOST CAPPED PLAYER:
Edwin van der Sar (130)

TOP GOALSCORER:
Patrick Kluivert (40)

Appearances in the finals of 1974 and 1978 represent Dutch football's most glorious moments in the eight World Cup competitions in which they have participated. It was during this period they were known for a brand of all-round play dubbed 'Total Football', but their solitary trophy win came in the European Championship in 1988, when they beat the Soviet Union in the final. The *Oranje* have come close on the world stage since, most notably in 1998, when they lost on penalties in the semi-finals. This time, in qualifying, they won all eight games.

WESLEY SNEIJDER

BORN: 09/06/1984
POSITION: Midfield
CAPS: 58
GOALS: 12

The Dutch playmaker was one of the stars of Euro 2008. He scored two goals, including an acrobatic effort against Italy later listed as one of the goals of the tournament. Sneijder was an unstoppable force going forward, a creative player who not only linked up with his attacking team-mates, but who proved his ability to find the scoresheet himself. He fell out of form after returning to Real Madrid and injuries meant he was in and out of the national side, but he returned to form following a move to Internazionale in 2009.

DENMARK

COACH:
Morten Olsen

WORLD CUP RECORD:
1986: Round 1, 1998: Quarter-finals,
2002: Last 16

MOST CAPPED PLAYER:
Peter Schmeichel (129)

TOP GOALSCORER:
Poul Nielsen (52)

A founding member of FIFA, Denmark had to wait until 1986 to qualify for their first World Cup competition. They arrived with a bang, beating two-time champions Uruguay 6-1 and qualifying for the last 16. There, they were knocked out by Spain, but their defining moment followed six years later, when they won the European Championship in Sweden. This will be the *Danish Dynamite's* first major tournament for six years – their fourth World Cup in total – after they failed to qualify for Germany in 2006 and the European Championship in Austria and Switzerland in 2008.

STAR MAN

NICKLAS BENDTNER

BORN: 16/01/1988
POSITION: Forward
CAPS: 31
GOALS: 10

The Arsenal striker scored three goals in nine games as Denmark qualified ahead of Portugal and Sweden from Group 1. He won the Danish Player of the Year award in 2009, the culmination of a meteoric rise through the Danish ranks. He scored three goals for the Under-16s in 2004, securing a move to Arsenal. He scored six goals in 15 games for the Under-17s and he was aged just 18 when he scored on his Under-21 debut in May 2006. Three months later he scored on his full debut in a 2-0 win against Poland.

JAPAN

COACH:
Takeshi Okada

WORLD CUP RECORD:
1998: Round 1,
2002: Last 16,
2006: Round 1

MOST CAPPED PLAYER:
Masami Ihara (123)

TOP GOALSCORER:
Kunishige Kamamoto (55)

Japan have won the Asia Cup three times in the last five years while qualification for South Africa ensures their fourth consecutive World Cup appearance. They failed to beat Australia in two attempts in qualifying, but comfortably emerged from a five-strong group. They made the last 16 in 2002, the only time they've reached the knockout stages, where they were eventually eliminated by Turkey, who finished third. The *Blue Samurai* disappointed in 2006 when they failed to make it out of the group stages. But now, boasting a mix of youth and experience, they will be looking to the knockouts.

SHINJI OKAZAKI

BORN: 16/04/1986
POSITION: Forward
CAPS: 20
GOALS: 15

The 23-year-old striker is still a relative newcomer to the Japan team, making his debut in October 2008. Okazaki made his biggest impact a year later, scoring two hat-tricks in six days. His first came against Hong Kong in an Asian Cup qualifier, which Japan won 6-0. The second followed within a week, against Togo, making it 14 goals in 18 games. The Takarazuka-born striker plays for J1 team Shimizu S-Pulse, for whom he had scored 29 goals by the end of 2009.

CAMEROON

COACH: Paul Le Guen

WORLD CUP RECORD:
1982: Round 1, 1990: Quarter-finals,
1994: Round 1, 1998: Round 1,
2002: Round 1

MOST CAPPED PLAYER:
Rigobert Song (130)

TOP GOALSCORER:
Samuel Eto'o (41)

Four-time African champions Cameroon had already qualified for the World Cup more times than any other African nation before they made it six in 2009. The *Indomitable Lions* lost their first two games but saw off challenges from Gabon, Togo and Morocco by winning four games in a row following the appointment of former Olympique Lyonnais manager Paul Le Guen. In 1982, Cameroon drew all three group games in Spain, but it was not enough to prevent them going out. In 1990 they reached the quarter-finals, where they were beaten by England.

STAR MAN

SAMUEL ETO'O

BORN: 10/03/1981
POSITION: Forward
CAPS: 90
GOALS: 41

This will be the Cameroon captain's third World Cup. In 1998, he was the youngest participant aged 17. Four years later, he scored his only World Cup goal when he hit the winner against Saudi Arabia. He netted nine in qualifying this time around, making him the highest scorer on the continent. Eto'o has won the Africa Cup of Nations twice and he is the all-time leading scorer, with 16 goals. At club level, for Barcelona, he won three La Liga titles and two UEFA Champions League titles.

ITALY

ITALIA

FIGC

COACH: Marcello Lippi

WORLD CUP RECORD: 1934: Winners, 1938: Winners, 1950: Round 1, 1954: Round 1, 1962: Round 1, 1966: Round 1: 1970: Runners-up, 1974: Round 1, 1978: Fourth place, 1982: Winners, 1986: Last 16, 1990: Third place, 1994: Runners-up, 1998: Quarter-finals, 2002: Last 16, 2006: Winners

MOST CAPPED PLAYER: Fabio Cannavaro (131)

TOP GOALSCORER: Luigi Riva (35)

Topping Group 8 in efficient style saw the holders continue their record of only having missed two World Cup tournaments. The *Azzurri* did not enter in 1930, but made up for it by winning in 1934 and 1938, becoming the first of two sides – along with Brazil – to retain the trophy. They failed to qualify in 1958 and were shocked by Korea DPR in 1966, but after losing in the final in 1970 they returned to winning ways in 1982. Three penalty shoot-out defeats in consecutive World Cups denied them further success. In 2006 they beat France in the final on penalties.

DANIELE DE ROSSI

BORN: 24/07/1983
POSITION: Midfield
CAPS: 51
GOALS: 8

A box-to-box midfielder with 51 caps for his country, Daniel de Rossi is one of Italy's most consistent performers. He was part of the side that won the World Cup in Germany in 2006, two years after he had helped the *Azzurrini* win the European Under-21 Championship. He made his full debut in 2004 and now poses a formidable presence in the centre of the park. He played nine games in qualifying but missed Italy's last game of 2009 after breaking his cheekbone in action for Roma, against Internazionale.

PARAGUAY

COACH: Gerardo Martino

WORLD CUP RECORD:
1930: Round 1, 1950: Round 1,
1958: Round 1, 1986: Last 16,
1998: Last 16, 2002: Last 16,
2006: Round 1

MOST CAPPED PLAYER:
Carlos Gamarra (110)

TOP GOALSCORER:
José Saturnino Cardozo (25)

Despite having won South America's showpiece tournament, the Copa America, on two occasions in 1953 and 1979, the *Albirroja* have failed to convert this form onto the world stage. They have qualified for eight of the 19 World Cup tournaments and made the last 16 on three occasions, although they were eliminated in the first round in Germany in 2006. South Africa will represent their fourth consecutive World Cup and at one stage in qualifying this time around, Gerardo Martino's side topped the group ahead of Brazil, raising hopes that this crop can cause an upset.

ROQUE SANTA CRUZ

BORN: 16/08/1981
POSITION: Forward
CAPS: 65
GOALS: 20

Despite missing much of the qualifying campaign through injury, striker Roque Santa Cruz poses Paraguay's biggest goal threat. He scored three goals in five games and managed to finish among the *Albirroja's* top scorers. Santa Cruz made his senior debut for Paraguay aged just 17. He scored seven goals as Paraguay qualified for the 2002 and 2006 World Cups. He joined Manchester City in 2009 after scoring 23 goals in 57 league games for Blackburn Rovers.

NEW ZEALAND

NEW ZEALAND FOOTBALL

COACH:
Ricki Herbert

WORLD CUP RECORD:
1982: Round 1

MOST CAPPED PLAYER:
Ivan Vicelich (71)

TOP GOALSCORER:
Vaughan Coveny (30)

New Zealand return to the World Cup for the first time since 1982, when the *All Whites* qualified for the competition for the first time in their history. They lost all three games in Spain, but just getting there represented a huge achievement for a nation more used to egg-shaped balls than round ones. Now, after competing in three Confederation Cup tournaments, they qualified for South Africa following a play-off win against Bahrain. Plymouth striker Rory Fallon scored the winner in a two-legged encounter. Four squad members play in England, while the majority play in New Zealand or Australia.

RYAN NELSEN

BORN: 18/10/1977
POSITION: Defence
CAPS: 40
GOALS: 8

Striker Shane Smeltz was the *All Whites'* top scorer in qualifying with eight and Rory Fallon grabbed the winner against Bahrain in Wellington, but when it comes to the tournament proper, defender Ryan Nelsen will be crucial. The 32-year-old is captain for club and country and he is a regular at the heart of Blackburn Rovers' defence, the only Kiwi to play in the English Premier League. He has 10 years' international experience after making his debut in 1999, against Poland.

SLOVAKIA

COACH:
Vladimír Weiss

WORLD CUP RECORD:
N/A

MOST CAPPED PLAYER:
Miroslav Karhan (95)

TOP GOALSCORER:
Szilárd Németh (22)

Slovakia's qualification for South Africa sees them involved in their first major competition since their participation as an independent state, which followed the division of Czechoslovakia in 1993. As yet, they have failed to emulate the success of the former state, who won the European Championship in 1976 and were beaten World Cup finalists in 1934, where they lost to Italy, and in 1962, when they were beaten by Brazil. Slovakia narrowly missed out on the tournaments in 1998 and 2002, but this time they topped a tricky group containing Slovenia and group favourites Poland.

MAREK HAMSIK

BORN: 27/07/87
POSITION: Midfield
CAPS: 29
GOALS: 8

Slovakian midfielder Marek Hamsik has become a target for Europe's top clubs following a series of impressive displays for club and country. A regular scorer for Napoli in Serie A, he played in eight of Slovakia's 10 qualifiers, scoring twice and linking well with top scorer, Stanislav Sestak. He scored again in *Repre's* 1-0 friendly win over the United States in November 2009 to take his total to eight in 29 games. Twice voted Slovakia's best young player.

BRAZIL

COACH: Dunga

WORLD CUP RECORD: 1930: Round 1, 1934: Round 1, 1938: Semi-finals, 1950: Runners up, 1954: Quarter-finals, 1958: Winners, 1962: Winners, 1966: Round 1, 1970: Winners, 1974: Semi-finals, 1978: Semi-finals, 1982: Last 16, 1986: Quarter-finals, 1990: Last 16, 1994: Winners, 1998: Runners-up, 2002: Winners, 2006: Quarter-finals

MOST CAPPED PLAYER: Cafu (142)

TOP GOALSCORER: Pele (77)

The most successful nation in international football, Brazil are the only team to have played in every World Cup competition. With five wins, they are also the most successful side and they have won the most games (64). They topped the South American zone and went 19 games unbeaten between June 15, 2008 and October 11, 2009. Coach Dunga skippered the side to victory in 1994 and he will be hoping to become only the second man after German legend Franz Beckenbauer to lift the trophy as captain and coach. Brazil hosted the competition in 1950 and will do so again in 2014.

KAKA

BORN: 22/04/1982
POSITION: Midfielder
CAPS: 75
GOALS: 26

The tournament in South Africa will be Kaka's third World Cup. He played just 25 minutes in 2002 in Japan/Korea, coming on as a substitute against Costa Rica in the group stages. Brazil went on to win the tournament but Kaka played no further part. In 2006, in Germany, he scored the winning goal in Brazil's first game, a 1-0 victory against Croatia. He was also named man of the match. More recently, he played 11 of *A Selecao's* 18 qualifiers, scoring five goals, the second highest in the Brazil squad.

KOREA DPR

COACH:
Kim Jong-Hun

WORLD CUP RECORD:
1966: Quarter-finals

MOST CAPPED PLAYER:
–

TOP GOALSCORER:
–

Korea DPR return to the world's top table after an absence of 44 years. In 1966 they finished in the last eight at their first attempt in the competition, drawing with Chile and beating Italy in the group stages and knocking them out in the process. They then took a three-goal lead against Portugal in the quarter-final but were eventually beaten 5-3. Now, having qualified for their second World Cup after narrowly missing out in 2006 in Germany, it will be the first time both North and South Korea will have competed in the same World Cup competition.

HONG YONG-JO

BORN: 22/05/1982
POSITION: Forward
CAPS: 11
GOALS: 9

After signing for Russian side FC Rostov in 2008, the 27-year-old became the only member of the Korea DPR side to play football in Europe. His experience sees him wear the captain's armband and his team-mates will look to him to create things going forward in South Africa. With coach Kim Jong-Hun building a solid foundation at the back, Jo provides the link between defence and attack. He scored from the penalty spot in the 1-1 draw with rivals South Korea in Shanghai, China.

IVORY COAST

COACH:
Vahid Halilhodzic

WORLD CUP RECORD:
2006: Round 1

MOST CAPPED PLAYER:
Didier Zokora (74)

TOP GOALSCORER:
Didier Drogba (40)

Les Elephants will be one of the youngest nations at the World Cup, but with a large number of squad members playing in the biggest leagues in Europe, they will make the short journey with high hopes. The Ivory Coast played their first competitive match in 1960 but had to wait 32 years for their first piece of silverware, when they won their first Africa Cup of Nations. After losing in the final of the same competition in 2006, they competed in their first World Cup later that year. Unfortunately they failed to qualify from a group containing Argentina, the Netherlands and Serbia and Montenegro.

DIDIER DROGBA

BORN: 11/03/1978
POSITION: Forward
CAPS: 58
GOALS: 40

After scoring the goal that secured top spot in Group E and subsequent qualification, striker Didier Drogba announced his side were capable of going all the way in South Africa. "It is going to be a challenge," he said. "My team-mates and I want to make history and change the way the world sees African football." Drogba topped the African zone goalscoring charts despite playing just five games. His move to Chelsea from Marseille in 2004 for £24million makes him the Ivory Coast's most expensive player.

PORTUGAL

COACH: Carlos Queiróz

WORLD CUP RECORD:
1966: Third place, 1986: Round 1,
2002: Round 1, 2006: Fourth place

MOST CAPPED PLAYER:
Luís Figo (127)

TOP GOALSCORER:
Pauleta (47)

Selecção das Quinas nearly missed out after a disappointing qualifying campaign that culminated in a nervy play-off win against Bosnia. However, their qualification completes their most successful decade in history, in which they have qualified for every major tournament. Portugal reached the semi-finals at their first attempt in the competition in 1966. They were beaten by hosts England, but forward Eusebio finished top scorer. They were eliminated in the first round in 1986 and 2002 but returned to form in Germany four years later, when they lost in the semi-finals to France.

CRISTIANO RONALDO

BORN: 05/02/1985
POSITION: Midfield
CAPS: 68
GOALS: 22

Cristiano Ronaldo missed five of Portugal's 12 qualifying matches, and it is no coincidence Carlos Quieroz's side failed to secure an automatic place without their talisman. That said, Ronaldo has struggled to replicate his scintillating club form while wearing international colours. He failed to score in the current qualifying campaign, but after netting 25 goals in his last season at Manchester United, he scored nine in six games following his record-breaking £80million transfer to Real Madrid.

SPAIN

COACH: Vicente del Bosque

WORLD CUP RECORD: 1934: Quarter-final, 1950: Semi-finals, 1962: Round 1, 1966: Round 1, 1978: Round 1: 1982: Last 16, 1986: Quarter-final, 1990: Last 16, 1994: Quarter-final, 1998: Round 1, 2002: Quarter-final, 2006: Last 16

MOST CAPPED PLAYER:
Ando Zubizarreta (126)

TOP GOALSCORER: Raul (44)

Spain head to South Africa as European Championship holders, and after winning all 10 qualifying matches confidence could not be higher as they look to win the World Cup for the first time. Their passing style of football and strength in depth make them many people's favourites to go all the way. After winning the European Championship in 1964, Spain ended a 44-year wait for a major international title when they beat Germany at Euro 2008. However, the closest they have come to adding the world's coveted prize was in 1950, when they finished fourth in Brazil.

DAVID VILLA

BORN: 03/12/1981
POSITION: Forward
CAPS: 54
GOALS: 35

David Villa has scored 35 goals for Spain and alongside strike partner Fernando Torres, he was *La Roja's* joint top scorer in the 2006 World Cup in Germany, with three. Villa netted six goals in qualifying for Euro 2008, becoming the first person to score a hat-trick in the tournament proper since Patrick Kluivert in 2000, when he bagged three against Russia. By the end of 2008 he had 12 goals to his name, becoming the first Spaniard to score six goals in six consecutive games.

COACH: Ottmar Hitzfeld

WORLD CUP RECORD:
1934: Quarter-finals, 1938:
Quarter-finals, 1950: Round 1,
1954: Quarter-finals, 1962:
Round 1, 1966: Round 1,
1994: Last 16, 2006: Last 16

MOST CAPPED PLAYER:
Heinz Hermann (117)

TOP GOALSCORER:
Alexander Frei (40)

Switzerland topped Group 2 in qualifying thanks largely to a run of five consecutive wins that followed a surprise 2-1 defeat against Luxembourg. Their appearance in South Africa will be their ninth at the World Cup finals and they'll be looking to go beyond the last 16 for the first time in 56 years. In 1954 they hosted the competition but were knocked out in the quarter-finals for the third time in their history. Despite a Josef Hugi hat-trick, they were beaten 7-5 by Austria. In 1934 they were knocked out by Czechoslovakia, four years later it was Hungary.

TRANQUILLO BARNETTA

BORN: 22/05/1985
POSITION: Midfield
CAPS: 49
GOALS: 6

Bayer Leverkusen's creative midfielder was one of two Swiss players to have featured in every qualifier as Switzerland topped Group 2. Still just 24 years old, Barnetta has already amassed 49 appearances since making his debut in 2004, aged just 19. This will be his second World Cup. In 2006, in Germany, he scored in a 2-0 win against Togo in a group match, but later missed a penalty when the *Schweizer Nati* were knocked out in the last 16 by Ukraine.

COACH:
Reinaldo Rueda

WORLD CUP RECORD:
1982: Round 1

MOST CAPPED PLAYER:
Amado Guevara (130)

TOP GOALSCORER:
Carlos Pavón (46)

Honduras will need to make it to the last 16 if they are to surpass the team that competed in the World Cup in 1982. There, *Los Catrachos* drew with hosts Spain and Northern Ireland, but failure to beat Yugoslavia in their last game saw them eliminated. A run of eight home games without defeat and seven goals in nine games from striker Carlos Pavon helped them qualify automatically this time around. A 1-0 win against El Salvador in their last match, coupled with a last-gasp equaliser for the USA against Costa Rica ensured their place at world football's top table.

WILSON PALACIOS

BORN: 29/07/1984
POSITION: Midfield
CAPS: 62
GOALS: 5

The 25-year-old powerhouse is a crucial figure for club and country. He made 16 appearances in Honduras' successful World Cup qualifying campaign to take his total number of caps to 62, while he has added some much-needed steel to Tottenham Hotspur's midfield following his move from Wigan Athletic in 2009. A hard-working and energetic midfielder with a formidable presence, Palacios can thwart opposing attacks and support his strike force at the other end.

CHILE

COACH: Marcelo Bielsa

WORLD CUP RECORD:
1930: Round 1, 1950: Round 1, 1962: Third place, 1966: Round 1, 1974: Round 1, 1982: Round 1, 1998: Last 16

MOST CAPPED PLAYER:
Leonel Sanchez (84)

TOP GOALSCORER:
Marcelo Salas (37)

Chile's qualification for South Africa sees them competing at the World Cup for the first time since 1998, when they were knocked out by Brazil in the last 16. They finished second only to Brazil in qualifying this time around, meaning they are more hopeful then ever of repeating the feat of the team of '62, their most successful in history. Competing on home soil, *La Roja* were beaten by eventual winners Brazil in the semi-final. They have competed in eight World Cups in all but have been knocked out in the first round in six of them.

HUMBERTO SUAZO

BORN: 10/05/1981
POSITION: Forward
CAPS: 41
GOALS: 17

Suazo scored 10 goals in qualifying to finish as CONMEBOL's top scorer, one ahead of Brazil striker Luis Fabiano. His domestic goalscoring record also makes for impressive reading. Since 2003, the 28-year-old has scored more than 200 goals. In 2006 alone, he scored 34 in all competitions, which made him the second highest scorer in world football. The Monterrey hitman has a knack of being in the right place at the right time and he played in 18 of Chile's qualifying matches.

ONE TO WATCH

You've read all about the star men, but here are 14 players also looking to impress this summer.

MICHAEL BALLACK

COUNTRY: Germany
BORN: 26/09/1976
HEIGHT: 1.89m
POSITION: Midfield
CAPS: 97
GOALS: 42

The German skipper has played in three European Championships, while South Africa will be his third World Cup. Germany have not lost a game when Ballack has scored since June 2005. A key player in the centre of midfield, he has racked up 42 goals in 97 appearances, four coming in the recent qualifiers.

GIANLUIGI BUFFON

COUNTRY: Italy
BORN: 28/01/1978
HEIGHT: 1.90m
POSITION: Goalkeeper
CAPS: 100
GOALS: 0

ITALIA
FIGC

One of the finest goalkeepers in the world, the Juventus stopper has been in excellent form for club and country and at 31, he is in the prime of his career. He has 100 caps and has played at two World Cups, including the *Azzurri's* triumph in 2006. He kept five clean sheets and didn't concede a goal in 453 minutes as Italy lifted their fourth World Cup title.

TIM
CAHILL

COUNTRY: Australia
BORN: 06/12/1979
HEIGHT: 1.78m
POSITION: Midfield
CAPS: 37
GOALS: 19

The attacking midfielder loves to get forward and averages a goal every other game for his country. Cahill may not be the tallest player but he poses an aerial threat and thrives at holding the ball up to bring others into play. He scored three goals in qualifying, including a brace against nearest rivals Japan.

JULIO CESAR

COUNTRY: Brazil
BORN: 03/09/1979
HEIGHT: 1.86m
POSITION: Goalkeeper
CAPS: 44
GOALS: 0

Described by his international coach, Dunga, as one of the best in the world, the Internazionale stopper conceded just nine goals in 16 qualifying games, pulling off a number of world-class saves as Brazil topped their group. Cesar was third-choice keeper in 2006 and so will be hoping to keep hold of the no.1 jersey this year.

LUIS
FABIANO

COUNTRY: Brazil
BORN: 08/11/1980
HEIGHT: 1.83m
POSITION: Forward
CAPS: 36
GOALS: 25

Fabiano scored on his international debut, against Nigeria in 2003, and won the Copa America a year later. He was left out of the side for three years following a dip in form, but after being recalled in 2007, he finished Brazil's top scorer with nine goals in qualifying. He scored two goals on four separate occasions.

STEVEN
GERRARD

ONE TO WATCH

COUNTRY: England
BORN: 30/05/1980
HEIGHT: 1.88m
POSITION: Midfield
CAPS: 77
GOALS: 16

ENGLAND

An inspirational player with bags of energy, Gerrard can play on the left, right or in the centre of midfield. This will be the Liverpool captain's second World Cup. In 2006 he finished England's top scorer, with two goals, and he has 16 in total. He scored three goals in England's qualification campaign.

ALBERTO GILARDINO

COUNTRY: Italy
BORN: 05/07/1982
HEIGHT: 1.84m
POSITION: Forward
CAPS: 39
GOALS: 16

ITALIA
FIGC

Italy's all-time top scorer at under-21 level, Gilardino has continued his record for the senior side, for whom he has netted 16 goals in 39 games. He bagged the equaliser that ensured the *Azzurri's* place in South Africa, against the Republic of Ireland. Four days later he scored a 13-minute hat-trick against Cyprus.

KLAAS-JAN
HUNTELAAR

COUNTRY: Netherlands
BORN: 12/08/1982
HEIGHT: 1.86m
POSITION: Forward
CAPS: 29
GOALS: 14

KNVB

ONE TO WATCH

'The Hunter' made his international debut in 2006, scoring two and providing two assists in a 4-0 win against the Republic of Ireland. At the end of the 2007/08 domestic campaign he left Dutch giants Ajax after scoring 76 goals in 92 league appearances. He scored 18 goals in 22 Under-21 appearances and has so far netted 14 in 29 internationals.

ANDRES
INIESTA

COUNTRY: Spain
BORN: 11/05/1984
HEIGHT: 1.70m
POSITION: Midfield
CAPS: 39
GOALS: 6

The tricky schemer was drafted into the Spain squad for the World Cup in 2006, but he was particularly impressive during their successful European Championship campaign in 2008. He forms a formidable partnership alongside club team-mate Xavi and he is considered one of the best players in the world.

FRANK LAMPARD

COUNTRY: England
BORN: 20/06/1978
HEIGHT: 1.82m
POSITION: Midfield
CAPS: 76
GOALS: 20

ENGLAND

A pivotal player in the heart of England's midfield, Frank Lampard has averaged a goal every four games, although he scored four in 10 matches during England's successful qualification campaign. Now in his 11th year as an international, this could pose the Chelsea star's last chance to lift the World Cup.

JAVIER
MASCHERANO

COUNTRY: Argentina
BORN: 08/06/1984
HEIGHT: 1.71m
POSITION: Midfield
CAPS: 55
GOALS: 2

After impressing for the Under-20s and Under-23s, Mascherano played every minute of Argentina's 2006 World Cup campaign. In 2008 he became only the second Argentine – after polo player Juan Nelson – to win two Olympic golds. He was awarded the captain's armband four months later.

FRANCK
RIBERY

ONE TO WATCH

COUNTRY: France
BORN: 07/04/1983
HEIGHT: 1.71m
POSITION: Midfield
CAPS: 41
GOALS: 7

FFF

The creative midfielder missed France's qualifying play-off win against the Republic of Ireland through injury. Ever since he made his international debut in 2006, against Mexico, he has continually impressed with a unique ability to unlock defences. Ribery has scored seven goals in 41 internationals.

FERNANDO
TORRES

COUNTRY: Spain
BORN: 20/03/1984
HEIGHT: 1.81m
POSITION: Forward
CAPS: 71
GOALS: 23

ONE TO WATCH

Injury has blighted the Liverpool striker's domestic season, but when fit he forms one half of one of the deadliest strike partnerships in international football, alongside David Villa. Torres is strong in the air and can score with either foot. His explosive pace makes him a nightmare to defend against.

NEMANJA
VIDIC

COUNTRY: Serbia
BORN: 21/10/1981
HEIGHT: 1.88m
POSITION: Defender
CAPS: 44
GOALS: 2

Vidic is a rock at the heart of Serbia's back line. In 2006, he formed part of a record-breaking defence that conceded just one goal in qualifying for the World Cup in Germany. More recently, the Manchester United favourite made eight appearances as Serbia qualified for the tournament in South Africa.

RISING STAR

Several players have launched their careers at the World Cup. Here are 12 more looking to follow in their footsteps...

SERGIO
AGUERO

After making his senior international debut, against Brazil in September 2006, the Atletico Madrid striker starred in the FIFA Under-20 World Cup in Canada a year later, winning the golden boot with six goals – and the golden ball as best player. Aguero has scored seven goals in 20 caps.

COUNTRY: Argentina
BORN: 02/06/1988
POSITION: Forward

STEFAN
KIESSLING

Striker Keissling joined Bayer Leverkusen in the summer of 2006 and made his international debut a year later. The 25-year-old is strong in the air and good with his feet, an excellent all rounder. He scored in each of his first five Bundesliga games in 2009/10.

COUNTRY: Germany
BORN: 25/01/1984
POSITION: Forward

MILOS KRASIC

The 25-year-old boasts remarkable composure on the ball. He also has good pace and movement, while his ability to play in the centre or out wide makes him a useful player for club and country. The CSKA Moscow star scored twice in qualifying and set up three in the decisive win against Romania.

RISING STAR

COUNTRY: Serbia
BORN: 01/11/1984
POSITION: Midfield

HUGO LLORIS

Hugo Lloris' impressive display in the play-off win against the Republic of Ireland was crucial as he kept the resurgent visitors at bay in Paris. The 23-year-old made several key saves for *Les Bleus*, and the Olympique Lyonnais stopper has won eight caps since making his debut against Uruguay in November 2008.

RISING STAR

COUNTRY: France
BORN: 26/12/1986
POSITION: Goalkeeper

JAMES MILNER

England boss Fabio Capello describes James Milner as "the future", but his performances for club and country in 2009/10 – including his senior debut, when he starred and provided the assist for England's equaliser in a 2-2 draw with the Netherlands – suggest he could make an impact this summer.

COUNTRY: England
BORN: 04/01/1986
POSITION: Midfield

GERARD PIQUE

After making his full debut in February 2009, Barcelona defender Pique has formed a burgeoning partnership with Carles Puyol. He has 13 caps and has scored four goals. In 2009, he became only the third player to have won the Champions League two years in a row with different teams.

COUNTRY: Spain
BORN: 02/02/1987
POSITION: Defender

RAMIRES

The 22-year-old midfielder was involved in his first World Cup qualifier when he came on as a substitute against Uruguay in June 2009. He now has 10 caps. An attacking midfielder with pace and energy in abundance, the Benfica starlet is strong in the tackle and has the ability to unlock defences going forward.

COUNTRY: Brazil
BORN: 24/03/1987
POSITION: Midfield

DAVID SILVA

Still only 24, it feels as though attacking midfielder Silva is older given he has been around for four years, and has already amassed 32 international caps for Spain. He made his senior debut against Romania in November 2006 and has scored six goals since.

COUNTRY: Spain
BORN: 08/01/1986
POSITION: Midfield

MIROSLAV STOCH

RISING STAR

Attacking midfielder Stoch found first-team opportunities hard to come by at Chelsea following his move from FC Nitra in 2006, but the Slovakian international has flourished on loan at Dutch side FC Twente. He scored one goal in three starts during the World Cup qualifying campaign.

COUNTRY: Slovakia
BORN: 19/10/1989
POSITION: Midfield

LUIS SUAREZ

RISING STAR

The 22-year-old striker boasts a remarkable goalscoring record. Since joining Dutch side Ajax in 2007, he has scored 57 league goals in 81 games. He has also smashed nine goals in 25 international matches, including five in the World Cup qualifiers after forming a prolific partnership with Diego Forlan.

COUNTRY: Uruguay
BORN: 24/01/1987
POSITION: Forward

CARLOS VELA

RISING STAR

Twenty-year-old striker Vela scored one and made another in the 4-1 win against El Salvador that ensured *El Tri's* place in South Africa. The Arsenal youngster boasts excellent composure in front of goal, while his awareness and passing ability allows him to bring his team-mates into play.

COUNTRY: Mexico
BORN: 01/03/1989
POSITION: Forward

THEO WALCOTT

RISING STAR

England's youngest ever player in a full international after he made his debut against Hungary in 2006, he was a surprise inclusion in England's World's Cup squad in Germany. In his second World Cup qualifier, against Croatia in September 2008, he became the youngest England player to score a hat-trick.

COUNTRY: England
BORN: 16/03/1989
POSITION: Forward

1930-2006
WORLD CUPS

England 1966

France 1938, 1998

Switzerland 1954

Spain 1982

USA 1994

Mexico 1970, 1986

Brazil 1950

Argentina 1978

Uruguay 1930

Chile 1962

This summer, South Africa will become the fifth continent to welcome the world's best footballing nations to their shores. Here, we look back at the previous 18 tournaments with a map revealing who hosted the World Cup and when...

Sweden 1958

Germany 1974, 2006

Italy 1934, 1990

Korea/Japan 2002

1930
URUGUAY

WINNERS: Uruguay

RUNNERS-UP: Argentina

HIGHEST GOALSCORER:
Guillermo Stábile (Argentina)
8 goals

NUMBER OF TEAMS: 13

TOTAL GOALS SCORED: 70

URUGUAY

MONTEVIDEO

DID YOU KNOW: The first goal in World Cup history was scored by Lucien Laurent. The Frenchman volleyed home after 19 minutes in a 4-1 win against Mexico in Group A.

1934
ITALY

WINNERS: Italy

RUNNERS-UP: Czechoslovakia

HIGHEST GOALSCORER:
Oldrich Nejedly
(Czechoslovakia) 5 goals

NUMBER OF TEAMS: 16

TOTAL GOALS SCORED: 70

MILAN
TRIESTE
TURIN
GENOA
BOLOGNA
FLORENCE
ITALY
ROME
NAPLES

DID YOU KNOW: Uruguay
remain the only champions
not to defend their title.
La Celeste didn't go to
Italy because so many
European teams said
Uruguay had been too far
to travel four years earlier.

1938
FRANCE

WINNERS: Italy

RUNNERS-UP: Hungary

HIGHEST GOALSCORER:
Leonidas (Brazil) 7 goals

NUMBER OF TEAMS: 15

TOTAL GOALS SCORED: 84

LILLE

LE HAVRE

REIMS

PARIS

STRASBOURG

FRANCE

LYON

BORDEAUX

DID YOU KNOW: Poland's
Ernst Willimowski is the
only player to have scored
four goals but finished on
the losing side in a World
Cup match. His team lost
6-5 to Brazil in Round 1.

ANTIBES

TOULOUSE

MARSEILLE

1950
BRAZIL

WINNERS: Uruguay

RUNNERS-UP: Brazil

HIGHEST GOALSCORER:
Ademir (Brazil) 9 goals

NUMBER OF TEAMS: 13

TOTAL GOALS SCORED: 88

BRAZIL

RECIFE

BELO HORIZONTE

RIO DE JANEIRO

SÃO PAULO

CURITIBA

PORTO ALEGRE

DID YOU KNOW: The World Cup final in 1950 boasts the highest attendance in the history of the competition, with 199,854 fans from Brazil and Uruguay packing into the Maracana in Rio de Janeiro.

1954
SWITZERLAND

WINNERS: West Germany

RUNNERS-UP: Hungary

HIGHEST GOALSCORER:

Sandor Kocsis

(Hungary) 11 goals

NUMBER OF TEAMS: 16

TOTAL GOALS SCORED: 140

BASEL

ZÜRICH

BERNE

SWITZERLAND

LAUSANNE

GENEVA

LUGANO

DID YOU KNOW: The quarter-final tie between Austria and hosts Switzerland is the highest scoring match in World Cup history. Austria won an enthralling 12-goal thriller 7-5 in Lausanne.

1958
SWEDEN

WINNERS: Brazil

RUNNERS-UP: Sweden

HIGHEST GOALSCORER:
Just Fontaine
(France) 13 goals

NUMBER OF TEAMS: 16

TOTAL GOALS SCORED: 126

DID YOU KNOW: Pele became
the youngest scorer in World
Cup history when he found
the net for Brazil against
Wales aged just 17 years
and 239 days. His 73rd
minute strike was enough to
separate the sides.

SANDVIKEN
VÄSTERÅS
ÖREBRO
STOCKHOLM
ESKILSTUNA
UDDEVALLA
NORRKÖPING
GOTHENBURG
HALMSTAD
BORÅS
HELSINGBORG
MALMÖ

SWEDEN

1962
CHILE

WINNERS: Brazil

RUNNERS-UP: Czechoslovakia

HIGHEST GOALSCORER:
Garrincha (Brazil), Valentin Ivanov (Soviet Union), Leonel Sanchez (Chile), Vava (Brazil), Florian Albert (Hungary), Drazan Jerkovic (Yugoslavia) 4 goals

NUMBER OF TEAMS: 16

TOTAL GOALS SCORED: 89

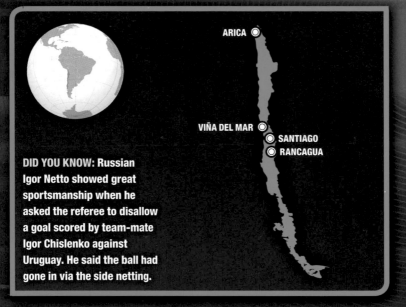

ARICA

VIÑA DEL MAR
SANTIAGO
RANCAGUA

DID YOU KNOW: Russian Igor Netto showed great sportsmanship when he asked the referee to disallow a goal scored by team-mate Igor Chislenko against Uruguay. He said the ball had gone in via the side netting.

1966
ENGLAND

WINNERS: England

RUNNERS-UP: West Germany

HIGHEST GOALSCORER:
Eusebio (Portugal) 9 goals

NUMBER OF TEAMS: 16

TOTAL GOALS SCORED: 89

SUNDERLAND
MIDDLESBROUGH

SHEFFIELD
LIVERPOOL MANCHESTER

BIRMINGHAM

ENGLAND

LONDON

DID YOU KNOW: The Jules Rimet Cup was stolen at an exhibition in March, just months before the competition kick-off. It was found by a dog called Pickles in some bushes in South London.

MEXICO

WINNERS: Brazil

RUNNERS-UP: Italy

HIGHEST GOALSCORER:

Gerd Müller

(Germany) 10 goals

NUMBER OF TEAMS: 16

TOTAL GOALS SCORED: 95

MEXICO

GUADALAJARA ◎ ◎ **LEON**

TOLUCA ◎ ◎ **MEXICO CITY**
◎ **PUEBLA**

DID YOU KNOW: Substitutions and yellow and red cards were introduced for the first time, but there were no dismissals. It was one of two tournaments – alongside Brazil, 1950 – to not feature a red card.

1974
WEST GERMANY

WINNERS: West Germany

RUNNERS-UP: Netherlands

HIGHEST GOALSCORER:

Grzegorz Lato

(Poland) 7 goals

NUMBER OF TEAMS: 16

TOTAL GOALS SCORED: 97

HAMBURG

HANOVER

WEST BERLIN

GELSENKIRCHEN

DORTMUND

DÜSSELDORF

FRANKFURT

GERMANY

STUTTGART

MUNICH

DID YOU KNOW: The 1974 World Cup was plagued by rain. Matches were played in muddy conditions. The game between West Germany and Poland saw the fire department called in to soak up the water.

1978 ARGENTINA

WINNERS: Argentina

RUNNERS-UP: Netherlands

HIGHEST GOALSCORER:

Mario Kempes

(Argentina) 6 goals

NUMBER OF TEAMS: 16

TOTAL GOALS SCORED: 102

CÓRDOBA
ROSARIO
MENDOZA
BUENOS AIRES
MAR DEL PLATA

ARGENTINA

DID YOU KNOW: Dutchman
Ernie Brandts scored at
both ends in Holland's 2-1
win over Italy in the second
round, making him the only
person to do so in the history
of the competition.

1982
SPAIN

WINNERS: Italy

RUNNERS-UP: West Germany

HIGHEST GOALSCORER:
Paolo Rossi (Italy) 6 goals

NUMBER OF TEAMS: 24

TOTAL GOALS SCORED: 146

A CORUÑA

GIJÓN

OVIEDO

BILBAO

VIGO

ZARAGOZA

VALLADOLID

BARCELONA

MADRID

SPAIN

VALENCIA

ALICANTE

ELCHE

SEVILLE

MÁLAGA

DID YOU KNOW: Hungary striker Laszlo Kiss is the only substitute to score a hat-trick – the fastest ever – in the World Cup. Hungary beat El Salvador 10-1, the biggest ever win in the competition.

1986
MEXICO

WINNERS: Argentina

RUNNERS-UP: West Germany

HIGHEST GOALSCORER:

Gary Lineker
(England) 6 goals

NUMBER OF TEAMS: 24

TOTAL GOALS SCORED: 132

MEXICO

⊙ MONTERREY

GUADALAJARA ⊙
IRAPUATO ⊙
⊙ QUERÉTARO
⊙ NEZAHUALCOYOTL
⊙ MEXICO CITY
TOLUCA ⊙
⊙ PUEBLA

DID YOU KNOW: Uruguayan defender Jose Batista received the quickest red card in World Cup history when he was sent off after just 56 seconds in a 0-0 draw against Scotland in the first round.

1990
ITALY

WINNERS: West Germany

RUNNERS-UP: Argentina

HIGHEST GOALSCORER:
Salvatore Schillaci
(Italy) 6 goals

NUMBER OF TEAMS: 24

TOTAL GOALS SCORED: 115

MILAN
TURIN
VERONA
UDINE
GENOA
BOLOGNA
FLORENCE
ITALY
ROME
NAPLES
BARI
CAGLIARI
PALERMO

**DID YOU KNOW: The
United Arab Emirates
players received a Rolls
Royce for every goal they
scored. They netted twice,
first in defeat against
West Germany and again
as they lost to Yugoslavia.**

1994
USA

WINNERS: Brazil

RUNNERS-UP: Italy

HIGHEST GOALSCORER:
Hristo Stoitchkov (Bulgaria),
Oleg Salenko (Russia) 6 goals

NUMBER OF TEAMS: 24

TOTAL GOALS SCORED: 141

BOSTON
DETROIT
NEW
JERSEY
CHICAGO
WASHINGTON DC
USA
SAN FRANCISCO
LOS ANGELES
DALLAS
ORLANDO

DID YOU KNOW: Oleg Salenko scored five goals and set up the other in a 6-1 win against Cameroon in 1994, making him the highest goalscorer in a single World Cup match.

1998
FRANCE

WINNERS: France

RUNNERS-UP: Brazil

HIGHEST GOALSCORER:
Davor Suker (Croatia) 6

NUMBER OF TEAMS: 32

TOTAL GOALS SCORED: 171

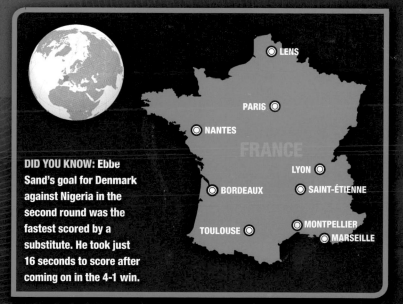

DID YOU KNOW: Ebbe Sand's goal for Denmark against Nigeria in the second round was the fastest scored by a substitute. He took just 16 seconds to score after coming on in the 4-1 win.

LENS

PARIS

NANTES

FRANCE

LYON

BORDEAUX

SAINT-ÉTIENNE

TOULOUSE

MONTPELLIER

MARSEILLE

2002
KOREA/JAPAN

WINNERS: Brazil

RUNNERS-UP: Germany

HIGHEST GOALSCORER:
Ronaldo (Brazil) 8

NUMBER OF TEAMS: 32

TOTAL GOALS SCORED: 161

SEOUL
INCHEON
SUWON
DAEJEON
DAEGU
JEONJU
ULSAN
GWANGJU
BUSAN
SAPPORO
RIFU
NIIGATA
KASHIMA
SAITAMA
YOKOHAMA
KOBE
FUKUROI
OSAKA
SEOGWIPO
OITA

DID YOU KNOW:
Turkey striker Hakan Sukur scored the fastest goal in World Cup history when he took just 11 seconds to find the net against South Korea in the third place play-off.

2006
GERMANY

WINNERS: Italy

RUNNERS-UP: France

HIGHEST GOALSCORER:
Miroslav Klose
(Germany) 5 goals

NUMBER OF TEAMS: 32

TOTAL GOALS SCORED: 147

GERMANY

HAMBURG

BERLIN

HANOVER

GELSENKIRCHEN

DORTMUND

LEIPZIG

COLOGNE

FRANKFURT

NUREMBERG

KAISERSLAUTERN

STUTTGART

MUNICH

DID YOU KNOW: Marco Matterrazzi's equaliser for Italy against France in the final – the last goal scored in open play in the World Cup – was the 2,663rd goal in the competition's history.

LEGENDS

Remembering the stars of past World Cup competitions...

FRANZ BECKENBAUER

COUNTRY: Germany
BORN: 11/09/1945
POSITION: Defender
CAREER: 1965–1977
CAPS: 103
GOALS: 14

WORLD CUP RECORD
1966: Runner-up
1970: Third-Place
1974: Winner

Nicknamed 'Der Kaiser', Beckenbauer was a sweeper famed for bringing the ball out of defence. Confident on the ball and tactically astute, he was also a great leader, captaining West Germany in 50 of his record 103 caps. As well as winning the European Cup three years running with Bayern Munich, Beckenbauer played in three World Cups, reaching the final in 1966, the semis four years later and finally lifting the trophy in 1974. In 1990, he became the first man to captain and coach a World Cup winning side, as his West Germany team beat Argentina in Italy.

SIR BOBBY CHARLTON

COUNTRY: England
BORN: 11/10/1937
POSITION: Midfield/
                    Forward
CAREER: 1958–1970
CAPS: 106
GOALS: 49

WORLD CUP RECORD
1962: Quarter-finals
1966: Winner
1970: Quarter-finals

Charlton could play as an attacking midfielder or as an out-and-out striker and he excelled for club and country. Playing under Sir Matt Busby at Manchester United, Charlton won three league titles, an FA Cup and a European Cup in 19 years at Old Trafford. In 1966, he won the European Footballer of the Year Award before he helped England win the World Cup. He scored against Mexico in the group stages and netted two more in the 2-1 win against Portugal in the semi-finals. Charlton played 106 games for England and scored 49 goals, a record that still stands.

JOHAN CRUYFF

LEGEND

COUNTRY: Netherlands
BORN: 25/04/1947
POSITION: Midfield
CAREER: 1966–1977
CAPS: 48
GOALS: 33

WORLD CUP RECORD
1974: Runner-up

Described as the world's greatest player in the 1970s, Cruyff captained the Netherlands at the World Cup in 1974. The *Oranje* arrived on the world stage playing 'Total Football', a fluid system in which every outfield player could switch position. Cruyff was instrumental in the Dutch beating Argentina and Brazil to reach the final. The playmaker even won his side a penalty inside the first two minutes of the final, but hosts West Germany eventually triumphed 2-1. Three times European Footballer of the Year, Cruyff lifted the European Cup three years running with Ajax before coaching Barcelona to the trophy in 1992.

JUST
FONTAINE

LEGEND

COUNTRY: France
BORN: 18/08/1933
POSITION: Forward
CAREER: 1953–1960
CAPS: 21
GOALS: 30

WORLD CUP RECORD
1958: Third-Place

The record holder for most goals in a single World Cup, Fontaine only played in the 1958 tournament in Sweden because of injury to one of his team-mates. However, he took full advantage, scoring in every game and finishing with 13 goals. The Morroccan-born attacker had made his international debut in 1953 but was in and out of the team until he starred in Sweden. He played in the 1959 European Cup final for Stade Reims and scored 30 goals in 21 appearances for France before a broken leg led to his career being cut short at the age of 27.

GARRINCHA

COUNTRY: Brazil
BORN: 28/10/1933
POSITION: Forward
CAREER: 1955–1966
CAPS: 50
GOALS: 12

WORLD CUP RECORD
1958: Winner
1962: Winner
1966: Quarter-finals

Left out of the Brazil team in the first two games of the 1958 World Cup in Sweden, 'The Little Bird' - born with a leg defect - was called up as *A Seleção* progressed. The winger justified his inclusion by setting up two goals in the final, Brazil beating the hosts 5-2. The player who first perfected 'the banana shot' was selected again in 1962, where he helped his country reach another final, although he was sent off in the semi-final. He encountered his first and only defeat in 50 matches for his country when Portugal eliminated Brazil in the 1966 quarter-finals.

MARIO KEMPES

LEGEND

COUNTRY: Argentina
BORN: 15/07/1954
POSITION: Forward
CAREER: 1973–1982
CAPS: 43
GOALS: 20

WORLD CUP RECORD
1974: **Round 2**
1978: **Winner**
1982: **Last 16**

Argentine centre-forward Kempes was known for his late runs into the box. He failed to score during the World Cup in 1974, but 'El Matador' made up for it four years later on home soil. *Albicelestes* finished runners up in their group but went on to win the competition, thanks largely to Kempes' goals. The Valencia striker scored two against Poland in a 2-0 win, two more in a 6-0 victory against Peru and another brace in the final as Argentina beat the Netherlands 3-1. He finished the tournament as top scorer and won the Golden Boot award.

DIEGO MARADONA

COUNTRY: Argentina
BORN: 30/10/1960
POSITION: Midfield
CAREER: 1977–1994
CAPS: 91
GOALS: 34

WORLD CUP RECORD
1982: Last 16
1986: Winner
1990: Runner-up
1994: Last 16

Maradona became Argentina's youngest ever player when he made his full debut against Hungary in 1977, aged 16. He went on to play 21 games in four World Cups, including two finals. He captained his side to victory against West Germany in 1986, scoring five goals during the tournament in Mexico. Two came against England in the quarter-finals. His first, scored with his hand, is one of the most controversial in World Cup history. His second, where he dribbled from his own half, has been described as one of the greatest goals of all time.

GERD MÜLLER

LEGEND

COUNTRY: Germany
BORN: 03/11/1945
POSITION: Forward
CAREER: 1966–1974
CAPS: 62
GOALS: 68

WORLD CUP RECORD
1970: Third-Place
1974: Winner

The World Cup's second highest goalscorer with 14, Muller arrived on the world stage at Mexico 1970, scoring 10 goals in six games to top the goalscoring charts, including hat-tricks against Bulgaria and Peru. Despite scoring twice in the semi-final against Italy, West Germany were beaten 4-3. He picked up consecutive winners' medals, first in the 1972 European Championship and again in the 1974 World Cup, when he hit the winner in the final against Holland. Muller, who won three consecutive European Cups with Bayern Munich in the 1970s, finished his international career with 68 goals in 62 games.

PELÉ

COUNTRY: Argentina
BORN: 23/10/1940
POSITION: Forward
CAREER: 1957–1971
CAPS: 92
GOALS: 77

WORLD CUP RECORD
1958: Winner
1962: Winner
1966: Quarter-finals
1970: Winner

One of the greatest players of all time, Edson Arantes do Nascimento - Pele – scored over 1,000 career goals and is the only man to win three World Cups. He made his international debut aged 16 and became the youngest ever player to win the World Cup, in 1958, aged 17. He scored a hat-trick in the semi-final against France and two more in the final against host nation Sweden. He missed most of the action when Brazil defended the title in Chile in 1962 and again in 1966, but in 1970 he was back to his best, helping Brazil win another title.

MICHEL PLATINI

LEGEND

COUNTRY: France
BORN: 21/06/1955
POSITION: Midfield
CAREER: 1976–1987
CAPS: 72
GOALS: 41

WORLD CUP RECORD
1978: Round 1
1982: Fourth place
1986: Third place

Platini boasted a unique ability to open defences with his passing ability. The Frenchman appeared in the 1978 World Cup and scored against Argentina in a group game. France failed to make it to the Second Round, but Platini captained the side four years later and again in 1986, and on both occasions the side were knocked out at the semi-final stage. His finest hour came in 1984, when France won the European Championship. He scored nine goals in five games before lifting the trophy. He retired in 1987 after scoring 41 goals in 72 French internationals.

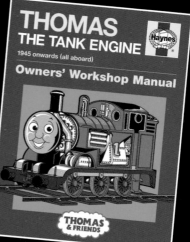